DIGGERS

Julie Dos Santos

This edition first published in 2010 in the United States of America by Marshall Cavendish Benchmark.

Marshall Cavendish Benchmark
99 White Plains Road
Tarrytown, NY 10591
www.marshallcavendish.us

Library of Congress Cataloging-in-Publication Data
Dos Santos, Julie
    Diggers / by Julie Dos Santos.
        p. cm. -- (Amazing machines)
        Summary: "Discusses the different kinds of diggers, what they are used for, and how they work"--Provided by publisher.
        Includes bibliographical references and index.
        ISBN 978-0-7614-4402-2
1. Earthmoving machinery--Juvenile literature. I. Title.
    TA725.D68 2010
    621.8'65--dc22
    2008054369

The photographs in this book are used by permission and through the courtesy of:
t=top b=bottom c=center l=left r=right m=middle
Cover Photos: Shutterstock; Inset: Shutterstock.
Title Photo: Photolibrary;
Content Page: Shutterstock

P4-5: Shutterstock; P6-7: BigStockPhoto; P7(inset): Misad/Dreamstime; P8-9: Mike Hutchings/Reuters; P9(inset): Q2AMedia Picture Bank; P10-11: Soundsnap/Shutterstock; P11(inset): Xalan/Shutterstock; P12-13: Shutterstock; P12(inset): Mel Stoutsenberger; P14-15: Midkhat/Shutterstock; P15(inset): Copyspace/iStockphoto; P16-17: Imagebroker/Alamy; P16(inset): Photolibrary; P18-19: Photolibrary; P19(inset): Stefanie Pilick/dpa/Corbis; P20-21: Bill Bachman/Alamy; P21(inset): Shutterstock; P22-23: Herrenknecht; P22(inset): Herrenknecht; P24-25: Axel Hess/Alamy; P25(inset): Photolibrary; P26bl: Q2AMedia Image Bank; P26br: Copyspace/iStockphoto; P27tl: Photolibrary; P27br: Stefanie Pilick/dpa/Corbis; P28-29: Shutterstock; P30-31: Shutterstock

Art Director: Sumit Charles

Client Service Manager: Santosh Vasudevan

Project Manager: Shekhar Kapur

Editor: Penny Dowdy

Designer: Ritu Chopra

Photo Researcher: Shreya Sharma

Printed in Malaysia
1 3 5 6 4 2

Contents

What Is a Digger?

Diggers come in many shapes and sizes. They do different jobs. Some diggers help build roads. Other diggers help farmers take care of their crops.

Diggers help people move dirt.

People use diggers to move dirt and rocks. Diggers have strong engines to move the heavy loads. Some diggers use shovels to dig. Some use big buckets to move dirt.

Bulldozers

Bulldozers work at building sites. They get land ready for building. Some bulldozers clear trees and rocks. Some move dirt. One kind of bulldozer works underwater!

Blade

Cab

Bulldozers use a large piece of metal, called a **blade**, to push dirt. The driver can move the blade up and down with a lever.

This bulldozer has a straight blade.

The bulldozer is moving sand.

Motor Graders

Many diggers work to build roads. One of them is a **motor grader**. It uses a large blade to make the ground flat. This prepares the ground for the concrete.

Cab

Motor graders can do other jobs too. Do you live where it snows? Motor graders move snow off roads in the winter.

This motor grader removes snow from a road.

Blade

The motor grader piles sand on a beach.

Tractors

Tractors help with many jobs on a farm. They can pull other machines such as plows. They can help get land ready for planting. Tractors have very strong engines.

Rear-view mirror

Wheel

Farmers put different tools on tractors. The tools change what the tractor does. One tool can mow grass. Another tool can pick crops. Another tool might dig dirt and plant seeds.

Tractors are strong enough to drive through muddy fields.

Tiller

The tractor uses a tiller to loosen the soil.

Excavators

Excavators dig rocks in mines. First they remove dirt. Then their large shovels take away the rocks or coal. After that, the excavators may put the dirt back.

This excavator is digging a huge hole.

The excavator can hold a lot of dirt in its shovel!

Most excavators use caterpillar tracks instead of wheels. Tracks let the excavators move on gravel or dirt. They keep these diggers from slipping.

Boom

Pivot

Bucket

Caterpillar tracks

13

Draglines

Dragline excavators use a big bucket. A thick cable is attached to the bucket. The bucket picks up dirt. The cable swings the bucket to drop the **load** far away.

Hoist cable

Boom

Bucket cable

This bucket is dumping a load of dirt.

Draglines are big and loud. One of the biggest draglines in the world is taller than twenty school buses! It is called Big Muskie.

Bucket

Inside the digger, an **operator** controls the cable and the bucket.

Bucket Wheel Excavators

Bucket wheel excavators are huge machines. An average bucket wheel excavator is longer than an airplane. This machine removes dirt and rocks in mines.

Bucket wheel excavators are very tall.

Wheel with buckets

The machine uses a big wheel with buckets. The buckets fill up with dirt. Then the wheel puts the dirt on a moving belt. The belt carries the dirt away!

The bucket wheel excavator uses caterpillar tracks instead of wheels.

Caterpillar tracks

17

Bagger 288

The world's biggest digger is the Bagger 288. This bucket wheel excavator scoops coal right out of the ground. It was made in Germany and is used in Europe.

Cables

Bucket wheel

Conveyor belt

Lights let people work on
the Bagger 288 at night.

This excavator is longer
than two football fields!
It weighs about as much
as ninety blue whales! It
only takes five people to
work this huge machine.

The wheel on the Bagger 288
has eighteen buckets.

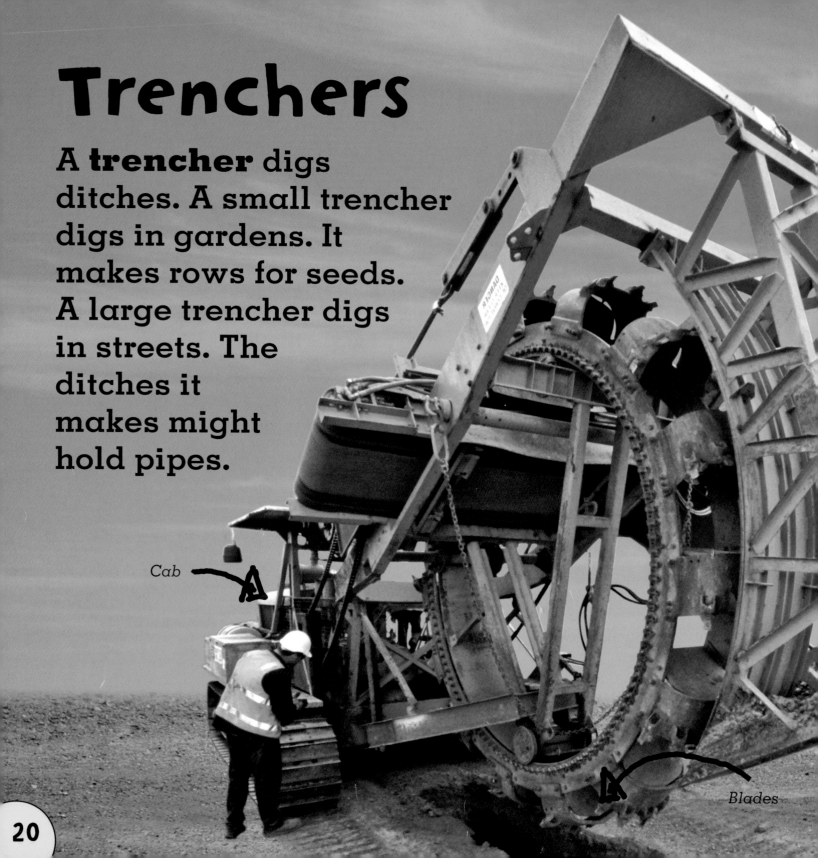

Trenchers

A **trencher** digs ditches. A small trencher digs in gardens. It makes rows for seeds. A large trencher digs in streets. The ditches it makes might hold pipes.

Cab

Blades

Trenchers that dig in soil use shovels to move dirt. Trenchers that dig in something hard use blades.

The blades on a trencher are very strong.

The bigger the trencher the bigger the engine it has.

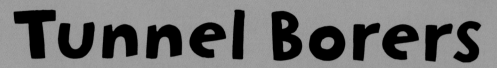

Tunnel Borers

Tunnel borers dig underground through dirt and rock. They dig tunnels in cities and in mountains.

Tunnel borers move through the earth like a worm.

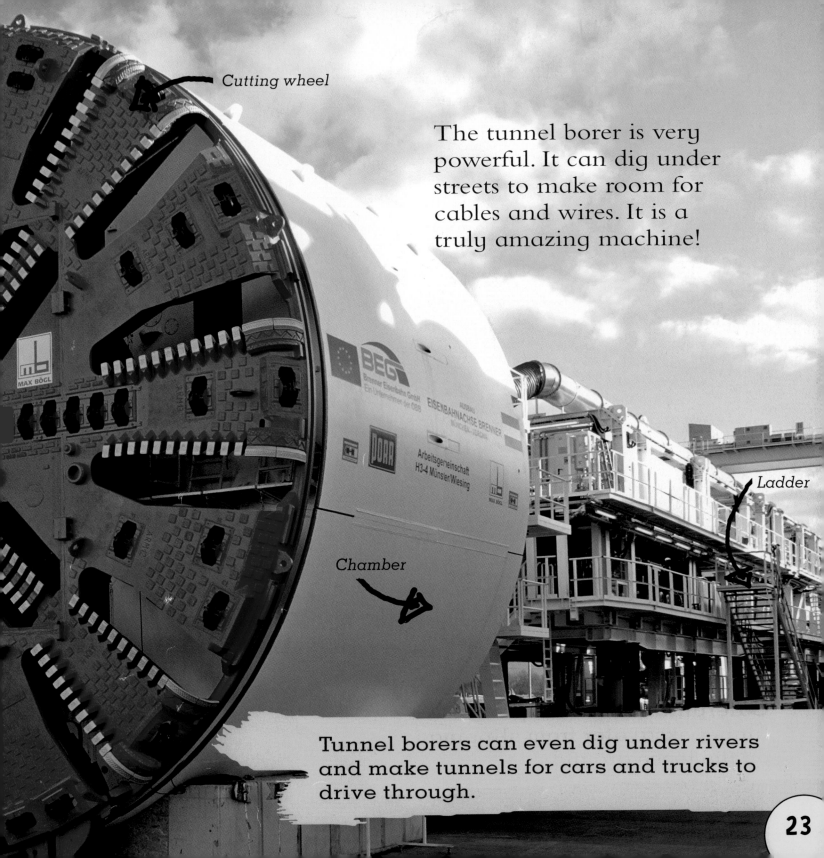

Cutting wheel

The tunnel borer is very powerful. It can dig under streets to make room for cables and wires. It is a truly amazing machine!

Ladder

Chamber

Tunnel borers can even dig under rivers and make tunnels for cars and trucks to drive through.

23

Tunnel Excavators

Tunnel excavators dig up large rocks. The excavators move the rocks. This makes room for tunnel borers to dig the tunnel.

Controls

Caterpillar tracks

Caterpillar tracks keep the tunnel excavator from slipping on the loose ground.

Tunnel excavators use big buckets and cutting tools. They dig through the hard rock. Some buckets are big enough to hold an entire family!

Arm

The operator uses the controls to dig and move rocks.

Summing Up

Diggers work in different ways. Some have shovels to scoop and lift. Some have blades that push. Some have buckets that carry dirt away. Diggers help us in many ways. Some help at building sites. Some help us build and fix roads. Some are used on farms.

Trenchers

Draglines

Bucket Wheel Excavators

Bagger 288

Amazing Facts

- Some bulldozers work underwater. They work by remote control. The driver can stay dry.

- The Chunnel is a tunnel that connects France and England. Tunnel borers took three years to dig 31 miles under the watery English Channel.

- The tires on the biggest bulldozer reach 12 feet tall. That is more than twice the size of most adults!

- **Most diggers are yellow. Yellow means** *be careful.*

- **The first bulldozer was built in 1923.**

Glossary

blade the part of a bulldozer that scrapes the ground

bucket wheel excavator a machine that uses buckets on a turning wheel to dig up dirt

bulldozer a machine that pushes sand, rocks, and dirt at construction sites

dragline a machine that uses big buckets to move dirt and rocks

excavator a machine used in mining to dig dirt and rock

load the material a truck or digger carries

motor grader a machine that smoothes the ground

operator a person who makes a digger work

tractor a machine used on a farm to pull other machines

trencher a machine that digs ditches

tunnel borer a machine that digs tunnels

tunnel excavator a machine that moves rocks to prepare for digging a tunnel

Index

Web Finder

http://www.kenkenkikki.jp/e_index.html

http://www.careervoyages.gov/students-elementary.cfm

http://www.activitytv.com/activity.aspx?actID=683&actTitle=683_Bulldozer&catID=5